Can I Have Some Chocolate, Please?

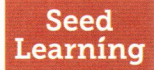

Can I have some chocolate, please?

Yes, you can.

You can have
some chocolate.

Can I have some cake, please?

Yes, you can.

You can have
some cake.

Can I have some chips, please?

Yes, you can.

You can have
some chips.

Can I have some rice cakes, please?

Yes, you can.

You can have
some rice cakes.

Can I have some yogurt, please?

Yes, you can.

You can have
some yogurt.

Can I have some biscuits, please?

Yes, you can.

You can have
some biscuits.

Can I have some wine, please?

No, you can't.

You can't have
any wine.

Let's learn about Ratha-Yatra.

June

Sunday	Monday	Tuesday	Wednesday	Thursday	Friday	Saturday
1	2	3	4	5	6	7
8	9	10	11	12	13	14
15	16	17	18	19	20	21
22	(23)	24	25	26	27	28
29	30	31				

Trace the word June
and circle the date.